Teaching Handwriting

A Guide for Teachers and Parents

by Jean Alston and Jane Taylor

A QEd Publication

First published in 1990 and revised in 1995

This edition published in 2000

© Jean Alston and Jane Taylor

ISBN 1 898873 12 7

Published by QEd, The Rom Building, Eastern Avenue, Lichfield, Staffs. WS13 6RN

Printed in the United Kingdom by Newcastle Instant Print (Newcastle-under-Lyme).

Contents

Introduction

Research has shown that many children have problems with handwriting. This can be a cause for concern for parents and teachers, and a source of confusion for affected children. *Teaching Handwriting* begins with questions that parents and teachers are likely to ask, outlines curriculum requirements for children at different stages of educational development, and suggests some principles which should be adopted if handwriting is to be taught successfully. The extensive list of resources allows parents and teachers to identify the aids their children require. The recommendations for handwriting correction, and the resource suggestions, enable parents and teachers to plan individual programmes for those who do not achieve handwriting success.

Guidelines for remedial measures are presented in the format of rules, ways in which problems can be avoided, and guidelines through which faults can be identified and corrected. The ten-point 'Rules round-up' can be used by pupils, parents or teachers, and provides a quick and concise method of ensuring that handwriting is progressing without pitfalls.

Jane Taylor and Dr Jean Alston provide a combination of expertise from the disciplines of psychology, education and occupational therapy. They both have extensive experience of working with children with specific and general learning difficulties. They are particularly interested in children affected by motor learning disorder (dyspraxia). They have helped many children with handwriting problems, and have written extensively on the subject.

Questions and Answers

Q: **Do many children have problems with handwriting?**

A: Yes, if a child in your care has handwriting problems this is not extraordinary. Many children have handwriting problems and the rules outlined here are designed to help them.

Research

1982   After at least four years of instruction . . . many children have still not acquired a level of competence in handwriting which is acceptable to their teachers.

(Rubin & Henderson)

1990   In International Literacy Year, it was estimated that four million adults in the United Kingdom have difficulty with reading and writing. Approximately 40 per cent of those with difficulties mention only difficulty with writing.

(Adult Literacy and Basic Skills Unit)

1991   20% of boys and 10% of girls hate writing.
37% of boys and 23% of girls write as little as possible or only when they have to.

(School Examinations and Assessment Council)

1992   While attention was being focused on the diagnosis and 'remedial' teaching of reading, the pressing need for similar work with reference to the teaching of writing has not been widely recognised. A 'WRITING RESCUE' programme would apply to a larger proportion of pupils than those who have difficulty learning to read.

(Cato, Fernandes, Gorman, Kispal & White)

1998   Within *The National Literacy Strategy* it was considered necessary to state very precise requirements for the teaching of handwriting. The following statement was included: 'Literate pupils should have fluent and legible handwriting.'

(DfEE)

The Curriculum

Q: **What does the National Curriculum require?**

A: The National Curriculum requires:

- 7 year-olds (Key Stage 1) to have a legible handwriting style.

  They should be able to:
  – write from left to right and from top to bottom of the page;
  – start and finish letters correctly;
  – write letters which are regular in size and shape;
  – have regular spacing between letters and words.

  Young children should be taught to:
  – hold a pencil comfortably;
  – write each letter of the alphabet.

- They should be taught the conventional ways of forming letters, both lower case and capitals.

- When letters are formed correctly, they should be taught to join letters in words.

- They should learn that, if they write clearly, others will be able to understand what they have written. *Year 2*

- The most able 7 year-olds will have handwriting which is joined and legible.

- 8–11 year-olds (Key Stage 2) to be developing legible handwriting in both joined up and printed styles.

- They should be taught to use different forms of handwriting for different purposes, e.g. print for labelling maps and diagrams; a clear, neat hand for finished, presented work; a fast script for notes.

- They should be accumulating a bank of words which they can write and spell correctly.

- At 11 years of age, the most able writers will have handwriting which is joined, clear and fluent and, when appropriate, is adapted to a range of tasks.

- At secondary school (Key Stages 3 & 4), pupils who have not already learned, should be taught neat, legible handwriting. Pupils who write in a joined and legible script, should be taught to write with fluency and, on occasion, speed.

- The most able secondary school pupils will have writing which is fluent, legible, and shows a clear grasp of the use of punctuation and paragraphing.

- In appropriate individual cases, pupils who have a disability which prevents them from using handwriting as a means of communication should be exempted from National Curriculum handwriting programmes of study.

- writing out the alphabet.
- finger spacing.
- using the map
   - Every movement.
      - Left
      - Right
      - Forward
      - Back.

      - Pushed
      - Pulled.

- Could use repeating sentence here.
   such as . . .

I pushed the car left and got to the __

Repeating - simple words.
          - changing harder selection of
                             words.
          Could even have harder words.
          there ready to cut out . . .
          then move onto writing once can read

A Model for Handwriting

There is no prescribed handwriting policy or script for schools in the United Kingdom. In most schools, a scheme marketed by a leading publisher is employed. Often the staff will have discussed the handwriting model they prefer, and the scheme will have been purchased. If a parent becomes concerned about his or her child's handwriting, it is important that the problem should be discussed with school staff. The pupil should be able to use the same handwriting model in both home and school.

Most commercially produced scripts have their strengths and weaknesses. Handwriting copy books are often not helpful, as some children may be able to create an accurate finished form, even when they are forming letters incorrectly. Showing the children how to form letters, e.g. so that they can copy the teacher's movements, is the best way to ensure correct letter formation.

The following handwriting model shows three scripts: The first is a simple script which has no entry strokes, but has exit strokes ready for joined writing. When letters become well formed, this script will allow the child to join letters in words easily.

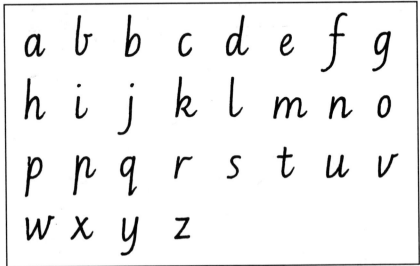

Letter forms for the child who is beginning to write

The second handwriting script has letters with entry strokes. Although this script is suitable for all writers, it is particularly suitable for pupils with specific reading, writing and spelling difficulties. Narrow loops are included. Lower loops on letters **f g j y (z)** are helpful, as their use allows pupils to make less pen-lifts as they write. Upper loops are optional and should be encouraged if the child finds the appearance of single strokes for letter uprights too difficult to achieve.

Letter forms, with entry strokes beginning on the writing baseline

Tasks

— Over highlighting pen — going over. , Dot to dot.
— Topics — Weekend, animals, interests etc.
— Make sure printed so understand.
— words / objects —
    Read and stick it on.
— Reading to find something — treasure hunt
    Tick words they can read.

— Draw, write down what it is,
— Tasting fruit and describing / touch

Some children are confused about when capital letters should be employed. Capital letters should be taught in the early stages of writing, and revised when pupils reach Year 2 or 3. At this later stage, the importance of capital letters for sentence beginnings, and to identify proper nouns, should be emphasised.

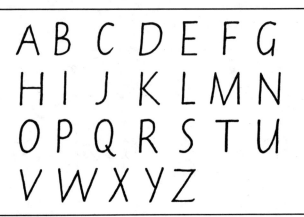

Capital letters for beginner writers and for teaching the use of capital letters

Punctuation.
Capital letter. Full stop.
Song to sing whilst writing.
'starting on this side of the page'.

'I' 'can' 'do' 'was'
                                                    'en'
Animals — Rhyming words. — 'sh' 'the' 'at'

Cat
bat ⟩ sentences and drawing.
sat   also drama.

Some Early Requirements

If a child is experiencing difficulties with handwriting, it is necessary to check that he or she is not affected by visual problems. For example, there may be binocular instability and/or convergence difficulties. This is sometimes the case when letters are reversed. Make sure that you consult an optometrist who has experience of children with literacy problems. A programme of eye exercises will often be sufficient to improve matters.

Correct movements for letter formation
A first requirement is that the student should have correct movements for letter formation. The 26 letters each have a consistent movement for formation, regardless of the handwriting model employed. If correct movements are not established at the beginner stage, problems occur as writing progresses, and there may be unnecessary handwriting difficulties for a number of years. Once correct letter movements have been established, the adoption of a joined script is recommended.

Letter exit strokes
It is recommended that letters which end on the baseline:
> a   c   d   e   h   i   k   l   m   n   t   u   x   z
should be taught with an exit stroke from the beginning.

Letter sounds and names
Writers need to be able to refer to the letters they write. If they know the sound or name of a letter they will feel more able to manage and control it. Sounds seem most suitable for the beginner writer and reader. However, letter names should be taught when conscious learning of spelling occurs. Letter names are always the same, and do not vary in the way that letter sounds vary. In some words, for example, there are letters which have no sound at all.

Alphabet Letter Cards are useful for teaching sounds, names and letter formations. The cards are just the correct size for small hands. The child feels in control of the letters, and is able to learn and manage them.

Lined paper for writing

Lined paper with broadly spaced lines is recommended for the beginner writer. Paper with three parallel lines for each line of writing is recommended when the writer begins to progress. The body of the letters should be placed on the baseline, 'x' height letters should reach the midline, and tall letters reach almost to the top line. Letters with descending strokes extend below the baseline. Line widths can be varied to suit the needs of the child, and according to what seems to be his or her normal writing size.

Example of three parallel lines

——— top line

-- midline

————————————————————————————————— baseline

Remember that children differ in their fine movements and coordination just as much as they do in speech and reading progress. A range of line widths should be available in each class.

Relative letter size

Letters

a c e i m n o r s u v w x z

are referred to as **mid zone letters**

Letters

b d f h k l t

are tall letters with ascenders

Letters

g j p q y (z)

are letters with descenders

Many poor handwriters do not appreciate that the bodies of letters should sit on the writing baseline, and that letters have different heights. Preliminary work, using wooden or plastic letters on a baseline, correctly, based on the forthcoming Rules 4 and 7, may be necessary before any correction of letter forms is undertaken.

Wooden letters to show the relationship of letters to the writing baseline

A script for joined handwriting
When a cursive script is employed, all letters end with an exit stroke. After each correctly formed letter, the exit stroke directs the pencil towards the beginning of the next letter. This helps the child to progress from writing individual letters to a script in which all or the majority of letters in each word are joined. The following guidelines are helpful.

1. Lower case letters which finish with an exit stroke from the baseline join diagonally. The letters which finish like this are:

    a c d e f g h i j k l m n q t u y x z

2.   Lower case letters which finish at the top join horizontally. Letters
        which finish at the top are:

o   r   v   w

3.   Letters **b   p   s** can also be given an exit stroke from where the
        letter ends on the baseline. This stroke will then join naturally to
        the next letter.

Letters **a   c   d   e   f   g   h   i   j   k   l   m   n   q   t   u   x   y   z**, if formed correctly
and with an added exit stroke, will join naturally to the next letter. A join
which must be taught is the *'over and back'* join, when a previous letter is
joined to letters **a   c   d   g   o   q**. This join can be observed in the words   *cat*
mat   hat   sat   and   land   sand.

If the teacher or parent wishes to observe letter joins easily and quickly, in
order to see where joins are incorrect, the student should be asked to write
the following words:

the   and   from   girl

Virtually all types of joins can be observed in the four words.

Posture
Make sure that the child is sitting comfortably, with paper tilted clockwise
for the left-hander, and anticlockwise for the right-hander. The writer's
forearm should be more or less parallel with the paper's vertical edge. The
non-writing hand should be used to hold the paper steady.

Pencil/Pen Hold
Pencil hold is important. If the child is taught to hold a pencil comfortably
in the early stages of writing, there is evidence that a conventional hold will
be established. When the forefinger, middle finger and thumb are employed
in a tripod hold from the beginning, preferably with the forefinger on top of
the pencil barrel, a dynamic pencil hold is able to develop. The dynamic

tripod hold allows the fingers and thumb to move freely, allowing a fluent handwriting style to follow.

The tripod hold needs to be developed very early. An incorrect pencil hold is difficult to change.

Handhugger Pencils and Pencil Crayons are suitable for encouraging an appropriate hold in young writers. LAMY pencils and pens are suitable for older pupils.

Handwriting – Key Words for Teaching

When children have begun to write and it becomes clear that they have problems, it is sometimes difficult to know where intervention should begin.

James writes about his best friend

All writers are likely to be able to write some words, however few. For example, despite considerable difficulty, James is able to spell the following words:

> *My   best   is   Darren   very   nice   he   play   in   a   spit-fire*
>
> *tank   too   I   go   with   he   and   have   their   up*

Confidence will be raised if James is shown that he spells these words correctly, and is then taught to write those words in a joined handwriting script. In this way, his written word bank is based on firm foundations. New words can be added to the word bank, and each can be written in the joined handwriting script.

Key Words have been identified by a number of researchers throughout the twentieth century. However, they were brought together in a formal manner by McNally and Murray in 1962. They identified the following groups of words as being the ones that readers and writers would most commonly need to use. The Key Words should be gradually incorporated into the pupil's written word bank.

Twelve words occur so frequently that they account for a *quarter* of the words we write:

a   and   he   I   in   is   it   of   that   the   to   was

The next twenty words occur with almost the same degree of frequency. These words should also be used for the teaching of joined handwriting.

all   as   at   be   but   are   for   had   have   him   his

not   on   one   said   so   they   we   with   you

Nouns should be taught according to the writer's needs. James has identified his own nouns: 'tank', 'Darren' and 'spitfire'. He would like to be able to write the following nouns:

friend   war   rifle   knife

We should teach him these words to help him to raise his confidence for writing and ultimately to raise his self-esteem.

Handwriting Rules and Conventions

Good handwriting has recognisable characteristics, which we refer to here as rules. For example, handwriting should be neither too big nor too small, and the uprights should slope in a uniform manner.

Readers should begin by examining the handwriting samples (a) to (i), and should attempt to identify the major fault in each sample. The answers to this exercise are on page 20.

Rules are an easy way of helping teachers, therapists, parents and children to avoid or correct poor handwriting. Each rule presented here has examples of handwriting in which the rule has been broken, some teaching points through which the problem might have been avoided, and a list of ways in which the problem can be rectified.

Rules help the child and adult to establish areas of difficulty. Every piece of handwriting has something good about it. Use the rules to find out what the good aspects are, and use them to praise the child before teaching and correction begin.

When handwriting is being corrected, rules should be presented in an order of priority to suit each individual. Only one rule at a time should be applied. Once it has been understood and becomes used automatically, the next rule can be introduced.

(a) He has green stripes on his Football boot.

(b) and is brother as got a BMX bike

(c) When we pull up on our drive in the car he always looks out of the window,

(d) are some of there David seman Lee.

(e) playing football

(f) Mummy oqehed the Parces

(g) Me and my mate fell faclled.

(h) have blue eyes I am small

(i) My dad and sam counch

Writing samples: some major faults

a.   Letters and letter parts are of different sizes.
Small **g, p,** stand on the line. Capital **F** and **T** are incorrectly employed.

b.   Letter bodies are not on the baseline.
Letters **a b d g k** are incorrectly formed.

c.   Writing is too small.

d.   Writing is too large.

e.   The slope of the letter uprights is irregular. The slope in the first word differs greatly from the slope in the second word.

f.   Letters and words are unevenly spaced.
p is reversed on one occasion.
Capital **P** is used inappropriately on one occasion.
Many letter forms need to be corrected.

g.   Help with diagonal and horizontal joins is required.

h.   Words are too close together.

i.   Rounded parts of **a d o** are not closed.

Rules and Recommendations

RULE 1 – Letter formation

This rule may need some adaptation to suit the model or style employed.

Small letters except d and e start at the top (d and e start at the mid point of the letter height)

or (if you are using a joined cursive script)

The entry stroke to each small letter begins on the baseline.

Problems with letter formation can usually be avoided if:

1. Parents are given letter formation sheets by the headteacher, before the child begins school.

2. A baseline is used from the early stages of writing.

3. Each child is taught correct letter starting points when he or she begins to write. (Drawing and 'pretend writing' should not be discouraged, of course, but when the child shows an interest in beginning to write, correct letter formation should be emphasised.)

4. Checks on letter formation are made at regular intervals, particularly during the early years of school, or until correct letter formation is well established.

This 8 year-old girl has problems with letter formation.

One day the sheriff thought of a plot to catch Robin Hood to make a game up

Here are some ways we can help her

1. Check her letter knowledge. Does she know the sound of each letter of the alphabet? A sound or name for each letter helps her to identify them. Letter sounds and names can be taught quickly, using Alphabet Letter Cards.

2. Introduce the Rule 4 concept (see page 28): *All similar letters are the same height.*

3. Sort plastic or wooden lower case letters into three groups:
   i) mid zone letters
   ii) tall letters (letters with ascenders)
   iii) letters with tails (letters with descenders).

4. Rule a line across a sheet of A4 paper placed in 'landscape' direction. Work with one of the above groups of letters. Ask the child to arrange the letters with the body of the letters sitting correctly on the line.

5. Introduce a cursive (ready for joining) handwriting script.

6. Introduce and ask the child to repeat Rule 1, either:
   i) 'Small letters except *d* and *e* start at the top', or
   ii) 'The entry stroke to each small letter begins on the baseline.'

7. Use writing paper which has three parallel lines for each line of writing.

8. Work on one letter at a time from the **i** family (**i t l**), beginning with **i** and stressing:
   i) letter entry strokes move diagonally from the baseline
   ii) letter exit strokes move diagonally from the baseline
   iii) similarities and differences between the letters in the **i t l** group
   iv) the relative heights of the three letters.

9. Work with one letter at a time from the 'hump' family of letters, **n m r p h b**, beginning with **n**, and stressing:

    i)   the entry stroke followed by the letter (this should help to improve the initial stabilising stroke of these letters, which is lacking in this child's writing)

    ii) the relative heights of the letters

    iii) the similarities and differences between each letter, compared with other letters in the same letter family

    iv) the need to make the down strokes parallel (Rule 3)

    v)   **r** is a difficult letter and needs much practice.

This girl starts the letter **o** at the 7 o'clock position, and **d** is incorrectly formed.

10. Work on one letter at a time from the 'rounded' family of letters, starting with the letter **c**, and stressing:

    i)   the starting point of the letter **c**

    ii) how each letter is similar and different from other letters in the group

    iii) the relative heights of the four letters **a c d g**

    iv) this girl starts the letter *o* at the 7 o'clock position, and **d** is incorrectly formed.

Plastic/wooden letters on a line and in alphabet arc help children to control the letters of the alphabet

RULE 2 – Letter formation and closure
Rounded letters are formed in an anticlockwise direction and should be closed.

Problems with letter direction and closure can usually be avoided if:

1. Each child is taught correct letter starting points when he or she first begins to write.

2. Attention is drawn to the rounded letters **c a d g** (**q** can be omitted at this stage and can be introduced later as the letter string **qu**).

3. The anticlockwise direction of letters is emphasised.

4. Regular checks are made on anticlockwise letter movements.

5. Regular checks are made on letter closure.

This 8 year-old boy has problems with letter direction and closure.

> a clown has
> Long shoes and red hair. and a clown is
> very funny. a clown has lots of things up
> his sleeve. a clown works in a circus and
> makes every body laugh. a Clown

Here are some ways we can help him

1. Introduce and ask the child to repeat Rule 2, i.e. 'Rounded letters are formed in an anticlockwise direction and should be closed.'

2. Select the rounded letters from a set of plastic or wooden lower case letters.

3. Use three-lined writing paper.

4. Introduce a cursive script.

5. Work on one letter at a time from the rounded family of letters, starting with the letter **c** and stressing:
    i) the entry stroke followed by the letter
    ii) the letter is started at the 2 o'clock position, curves upwards to begin with, and is oval in shape
    iii) the similarities and differences of each letter compared with others in the letter family
    iv) the letters **a d g** must be closed. To get this correct, begin the letter well to the right before you move the pencil left, ensure that it has a definite 'cap' on, and begin the upward movement (after the oval part), when the pencil reaches the 6 o'clock position.

RULE 3 – Letter slope
All down strokes are straight and parallel

Problems with irregularity of slope can be avoided if:

1. Writing patterns with regular uprights are taught from the beginning.

$$|_1|_1 \quad |_1|_1 \quad |_1|_1 \quad |_1|_1$$

2. Attention is drawn to the straight lines in the following letters:
   a b d f g h i j k l m n p q r t u y (w)

3. Attention is drawn to the parallel lines in the letters
   h m n u y (w)

4. The relationship between regular straight and parallel strokes and handwriting is emphasised throughout the early years.

He usually wears bright clothes. He
sits at a desk covered in Fan mail. His
helpers are beeth chequins, 'saagreen and
Crow and the children in the store. In the
morning he has in celebrities. His brilliant
programme starts at 9.00am and finishes
at 12 o'clock

This 10 year-old boy has writing with variable slope.

Here are some ways we can help him

1. Introduce and ask the child to repeat Rule 3, i.e. 'All down strokes are straight and parallel.'

2. Use plastic or wooden lower case letters to sort out all the letters which have one or more down strokes.

3. Use a ruler and mark with a red pen the lines which should be straight and parallel in the words 'bright' and 'helpers'. (Refer to similarly selected words for your own child/pupil.) Ask the child to comment on the lines drawn, bearing in mind Rule 3.

4. Use three-lined writing paper.

5. Practise the straight line pattern above.

6. Work on one letter at a time, beginning with letters with parallel lines within them, e.g. **n** or **u**.

Problems with irregularity of letter height or size can usually be avoided if:

1. Writing paper with a writing baseline is used during the early years.

2. Attention is drawn to the heights of different letter groups:

a c e i m n o r s u v w x z	mid zone letters
b d f h k l t	tall letters with ascenders
g j p q y (z)	letters with tails/descenders

3. Three-parallel-lined writing paper is introduced at a critical stage of early handwriting development.

This 7 year-old boy has problems with letter heights and sizes.

> He has got one Brother and one sister
> he has got ginger hair brown eyes
> puple Jumper and and his Brother
> I think gas this school and
> his sister is in the 4 year and
> his sister likes netball

Here are some ways we can help him

1. Introduce and ask the child to repeat Rule 4, i.e. 'All similar letters are the same height'.

2. Sort plastic or wooden lower case letters into three groups:
   i) mid zone letters

    ii) tall letters (letters with ascenders)
    iii) letters with tails (letters with descenders).

3.   Rule a single line (landscape direction) across a sheet of A4 paper. Work with one of the above letter groups. Ask the child to arrange the letters with the body of the letters sitting on the line correctly.

4.   Use three-lined writing paper.

5.   Introduce a cursive script.

6.   Begin by working on mid zone letters.

RULE 5 – Letter spacing
Letters within a word should be evenly spaced.

Problems with letter spacing can usually be avoided if:

1. Each child is taught correct letter starting points when he or she first begins to write.

2. The starting point for each letter is on the baseline, i.e. if a joined cursive script is adopted.

3. Graph paper is occasionally employed so that equality of letter size and spacing can be emphasised. Letters will fill the spaces of one or two squares. CORRECT LETTER SIZE AND CORRECT LETTER SPACING TEND TO GO HAND IN HAND.

This 6 year-old girl has problems with relative letter size and spacing.

Here are some ways we can help her

1. Introduce and ask the child to repeat Rule 4, i.e. 'All similar letters are the same height.'
2. Sort plastic or wooden lower case letters into three groups:
   i) mid zone letters
   ii) tall letters (letters with ascenders)
   iii) letters with tails (letters with descenders).

3. Introduce and ask the child to repeat Rule 5, i.e. 'Letters within a word should be evenly spaced.'
4. Use graph paper to show the even spacing of letters when the mid zone of each letter occupies a square. Begin with the mid zone letters.
5. The introduction of a cursive script allows one to show how letter entry and exit strokes help to regulate spacing between letters. Squared paper is particularly beneficial when a cursive script is employed.
6. Use three-lined writing paper.

Problems with word spacing can usually be avoided if:

1. The child is aware that letters are grouped to form words.

2. Words are on occasion presented on separate cards, as in the *Breakthrough to Literacy* reading and writing approach.

3. Small cardboard 'fingers' are available for the child to try out word spacing.

Sample A
This 8 year-old boy has word spacing which is unduly narrow.

> Kitt is covered with a bonded shell which can with stand any bullets. Michael helps people to beat os people who are trying to take over their business. I like the program very much and hope to see more like it.

Sample B
This 7 year-old girl has word spacing which is unduly large.

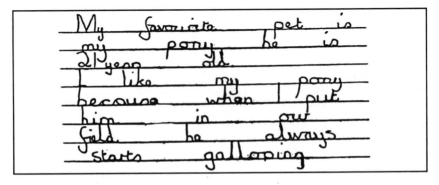

Sample C

This 7 year-old boy has letters and words which are unevenly spaced.

theguick brown fox jumpsover tlazy dog

Here are some ways we can help

Sample A

1. Introduce and ask the child to repeat Rule 6, i.e. 'Words should be evenly spaced.'
2. Ask the child to look at the first line to see if he notices anything about the spacing. Discuss the variation in spacing (in this case, between 'Kitt' and 'is' and between 'a' and 'bonded').
3. Ask him to look at the rest of the passage; he should put a tick in all the adequate spaces and a cross in the spaces which are too small.
4. Check whether he often leaves a small space after a full stop.
5. Ask him to write a few sentences concentrating upon the spacing. Correct spaces should be ticked and unduly narrow or unduly wide spaces should be marked with a cross.

Sample B

1. Introduce and ask the child to repeat Rule 6, i.e. 'Words should be evenly spaced.'
2. Discuss how much space should normally be left between words.
3. Make a cardboard 'finger' about the size of two of her letter 'o's.
4. Ask her to write out a sentence. Check the spaces using the cardboard 'finger'. Tick the spaces that are correct.

Sample C

1. Introduce and ask the child to repeat Rule 6, i.e. 'Words should be evenly spaced.'
2. Discuss how much space should normally be left between words.
3. Make a cardboard 'finger' about the size of two letter 'o's.
4. Use the cardboard finger to help with word spacing.
5. Use three-lined writing paper.
6. Introduce a cursive script.

RULE 7 – Letter/word alignment
The body of the letter sits on the line.

Problems with letter and word alignment can usually be avoided if:

1. Writing paper with a baseline is used during the early years.

2. Attention is drawn to the fact that the body of each letter sits on the baseline.

This 9 year-old boy has problems in placing letters on the writing baseline and with the relative heights of letters.

> and he has got a red bike and is brother as got a
> Bmx bike it is yellow and blue and is dad plays football
> and Davids brother plays foot boll as well Davids dad
> as got a gold racher and it as got Ten gears and
> big weels and it as got black weels and Davids
> bike as got 3 gears on is bike and he plays cwosn
> as well

Here are some ways we can help him

1. Sort plastic or wooden lower case letters into three groups:
    i) mid zone letters
    ii) tall letters (letters with ascenders)
    iii) letters with tails (letters with descenders)
2. Introduce and ask the child to repeat Rule 7, i.e. 'The body of the letter sits on the line.'
3. Work with one of the above groups of letters, placing the letters on the baseline correctly (allow the pupil to choose the first group of letters for attention).
4. Use three-lined writing paper.
5. Consider introducing the use of a cursive script. (Note that writing speed would be reduced for a short period of time.)

RULE 8 – Letter joins
Letters which finish at the top join horizontally.

Problems with horizontal letter joins can be avoided if:

1. Attention is drawn to those letters which are followed by a horizontal join, i.e.   o   r   v   w   (f).

2. Checks on horizontal joins are made at regular intervals.

This 13 year-old boy has difficulty with horizontal joins

> Same bus had just come to fight. they
> had of Boots, are had a knife same
> had Bells A fight started at the Back.
> We wanted to get allay. there was no
> way out, same kids ran an the field
> Sameone threw a Ball.

Here are some ways we can help him

1. Introduce and ask the child to repeat Rule 8, i.e. 'Letters which finish at the top join horizontally.'
2. Use three-parallel-lined writing paper.
3. Practise each letter which has a horizontal exit stroke.
4. Consider the length of the exit stroke; **a r v w (t)** followed by **i u** or **y** will have exit strokes shorter than when they are followed by **a** or **o**. The stroke has to be extended when it is followed by a rounded letter.
5. Begin work on 'wi' followed by 'wa' and 'wo'.

> **RULE 9 – Letter joins**
> *Letters which finish at the bottom join diagonally.*

Problems with diagonal joins can be avoided if:

1. Letters are taught with exit strokes from the baseline ready for the ligature/next entry stroke.

2. Checks on diagonal joins are made at regular intervals.

3. Letter entrance strokes begin on the baseline, as in a joined cursive script.

This 13 year-old boy has difficulty with diagonal joins.

Here are some ways we can help him

1. Introduce and ask the child to repeat Rule 8, i.e. 'Letters which finish at the bottom join diagonally.'
2. Use three-lined writing paper.
3. Work on the formation and relative heights of letters.
4. Concentrate on the entry and exit strokes of letters with diagonal joins.

RULE 10 – Sentence formation
Each sentence begins with a capital letter and ends with a full stop.

Problems with sentence formation can usually be avoided if:

1. It can be shown that each oral statement can form a sentence. Each statement then begins with a capital letter and ends with a full stop.

2. A statement can be written on one strip of paper to indicate the sentence unit.

3. Regular checks are kept on sentence formation.

4. Particular attention is paid to use of the word 'and'. 'And' is used to join two statements to make one sentence; it should not be overused.

This 8 year-old boy has difficulty with forming sentences.

> my best friend
> is David he has singer hair and brown eyes and freckles
> and he likes football as well and he is wearing a
> green Jumper and brown Trousers and he is wearing
> brown socks and brown shoes and a white tea shirt

This 7 year-old girl has difficulty with forming sentences. She also places the full stop incorrectly.

> I like Joanna. Because she is my
> friend. And she has a blue
> cardigan. And she has blonde
> Hair. And she has blue eyes.
> And she has a brown
> dress with flowers on it.

Here are some ways we can help them

1. Introduce and ask the child to repeat Rule 10, i.e. 'Each sentence begins with a capital letter and ends with a full stop.'
2. Discuss the use of the capital letter for beginning a sentence.
3. Discuss the use of the capital letter for a proper noun/name.
4. Ensure that the child understands that capital letters are not used just because the writing continues on a new line.
5. Look at the writing and decide if a word should be left out and replaced with a full stop, e.g. in the overuse of 'and'.
6. Ensure that the full stop is positioned correctly, i.e. on the baseline immediately after the last letter of the sentence.
7. Ensure that sufficient space is left between the full stop and the capital letter of the next sentence.

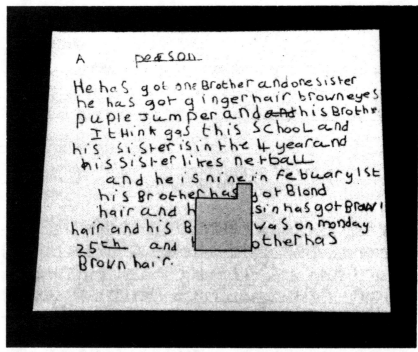

Cardboard finger showing spacing

Rules Round-up: Ten-Point Plan

IF YOU ARE USING A PRINT SCRIPT

1. Small letters except **d** and **e** start at the top.

or

IF YOU ARE USING A JOINED CURSIVE SCRIPT

1. The entry stroke to each small letter begins on the baseline.

2. Rounded letters are formed in an anticlockwise direction and should be closed.

3. All down strokes are straight and parallel.   [SLOPE]

4. All similar letters are the same height.   [SIZE]

5. Letters within a word should be evenly spaced.   [SPACE]

6. Words should be evenly spaced (spaces between words should be approximately the size of two 'o's of the person's writing).   [SPACE]

7. The body of the letter sits on the line.   [SITTING ON THE LINE]

8. Letters which finish at the top join horizontally.

9. Letters which finish at the bottom join diagonally.

10. Each sentence should begin with a capital letter and finish with a full stop.

Although all rules are important if you are to develop a high standard of legibility, remembering the FOUR Ss will take you some way towards achieving your aim.

   The four Ss SLOPE
           SIZE
           SPACE
           SITTING ON THE LINE

Useful Resources

Handwriting involves much more than letters, words and sentences on paper. It requires good posture, penhold, paper position and the provision of appropriate materials. Materials presented in this list will be useful for many children.

The choice of materials will influence outcome. An H pencil produces a fainter line than an HB pencil. Nib or tip width, or colour of ink, will alter the appearance of the writing. The use of lined paper can have a dramatic effect on the overall appearance of writing. It influences letter and word alignment, the understanding of how heights of letters and letter parts relate to each other, and how they all relate to the baseline.

Parents and teachers should encourage children to look carefully at how they sit when they write, and how they hold a pencil or pen. They should observe how the hand and forearm are used for writing, and ensure that lighting does not cast a shadow on the writing surface.

Pencils
B pencils are softer and make good contact with paper. Their use prevents the thin grey line that often results from use of a harder pencil. However, a variety of pencils should be available. Pupils pressing heavily as they write might prefer and profit from a harder H or HB lead.

Handhugger Pencils and *Pencil Crayons* have a triangular barrel which encourages conventional pencil hold. The barrels have a matt finish to prevent fingers from slipping.

LAMY Pencils have a triangular hold position, and are suitable for children of 7+ years.

Pens
It is useful to select from a wide variety of pens. Some pupils may well prefer what others would reject. However, there are some things to avoid,

such as metallic slippery barrels, which tend to encourage an excessively firm grip and may also lead to extra pressure between pen and paper surface. Always ask the shop assistant if you are able to try out the pen before purchase.

LAMY Pens have a triangular hold position, and are suitable for children of 7+ years. With some children they are able to correct inappropriate penhold. W.H. Smith cartridge pen has a rubberised penhold section.

Pencil and Pen Holders
Additional grips can sometimes be used to establish, modify or correct pencil and pen hold. Early Learning Centres have holders with small animal heads which many young children enjoy using. Grippy and triangular pencil holders are available from Learning Development Aids.

Fluorescent Pens
A fluorescent pen can be used to draw attention to the writing baseline, to assist pupils who find writing on lines difficult.

Letters
Children should feel in complete control of letters. They should be able to say the letter sounds for reading and early writing, and say letter names when they become consciously involved in learning to spell. Letter cards, or wooden or plastic letters, allow the child to handle and become familiar with all letters of the alphabet. Placing the letters in an alphabetical arc, as on page 23, provides the foundation for a range of activities to develop alphabet skills. For example, the pupil can be asked to replace letters which the teacher has withdrawn from the sequence. Alternate letters can be withdrawn and replaced. The vowels can be withdrawn and memorised.

Alphabet Letter Cards incorporate all the skills of letter management.

Galt Plywood Script and *Capital Letters* give adequate tactile experience.

Writing Paper

It is helpful to teach handwriting on lined paper. Widely spaced lines are suitable for most young children. In the early stages, the child may not write on lines provided, but may write between them. However, he or she does need to know that each letter has a relationship to the baseline. Many letters sit on the baseline and some, such as **g   p   y**, descend below it. The beginner writer can be provided with paper which has only one or two lines on the whole sheet. Gradually, as writing size reduces, and the writer becomes more competent, the number of lines can be increased, and the spaces between them reduced.

Lines can be provided simply for letter and word baselines, or for the separate letter parts. Paper can be obtained in two, three or four tramlined formats, which show the writer the relative sizes of different letter groups. The size of the child's normal writing will help the parent or teacher to select lined paper of appropriate dimensions. Teachers should note that children differ greatly in their degree of coordination and fine motor skills. Lined paper is particularly helpful for those children who are less competent in this respect. A range of lined paper formats should be available in each classroom.

Taskmaster Ltd supply Right Line paper, which has tactile lines. This is expensive, but could be laminated for repeated use with water-based marker pens.

Paper can be used in portrait (vertical) or landscape (horizontal) direction. Young children can reach the top easily when paper is in landscape position. The left to right writing convention is also encouraged by landscape paper position.

Sloping Boards

Many pupils have poor posture, rest their heads near to the paper surface, or peer too closely as they write. It is always advisable to seek advice from an optometrist experienced in dealing with children with literacy difficulties, who is likely to be aware of the visual problems these children are likely to experience. However, a sloping board will also help to alleviate problems.

Tables and Chairs

As a rule of thumb, the table should be half the height of the child, and the chair one-third of the height of the child (left-handers should be seated a little higher than their right-handed classmates). Discarded telephone directories can be used to raise the seat height. Feet should be flat on the floor, so shorter children would benefit from a box or stool on which to place their feet. Forearms should rest on the table, and the non-writing hand should hold the paper steady.

Dycem

Dycem is a matt-finished material which can be placed beneath paper or writing book, so that the correct position can be established. Corrected posture can be maintained by the use of Dycem.

Erasers

A good quality soft rubber is essential for good presentation. Many pupils do not know how to use an eraser. Make sure that they are taught. Repeated fine motor coordination movements are required for the use of an eraser. Some pupils will need specific instructions and practice of this task.

Rulers

Simple rulers can be used for underlining. There are special rulers for left-handed pupils.

Compasses

Cheap and flimsy compasses are difficult to use. You should check that the pencil holder is firm, and that the knob is easy to manipulate. Those who are less competent in fine motor function will need extra practice in using a compass.

Addresses for handwriting resources

Dycem
Nottingham Rehab Supplies, Novara House, Excelsior Road, Ashby Park, Ashby, Leicestershire LE65 1NG.
Tel: 0870 600 0197

LAMY Safari Pens and Pencils
The Pen Shop, 199 Regent Street, London W1R 7WA.
The Pen Shop, 54 King Street, Manchester M2 4LY.
Postal sales – Tel: 0161 839 3966

Plywood Letters: Capital and Script
Galt Educational, Culvert Street, Oldham, Lancashire OL4 2ST
Tel: 0161 627 0795
Email: enquiries@galt-educational.co.uk

Sloping Boards
Philip and Tacey Ltd., Northway, Andover, Hampshire SP10 5BA.
Tel: 01264 332 171
Email: sales@philipandtacey.co.uk
Children's Seating Centre, Whitcomb Street, London WC2H 7HA.

W.H. Smith Cartridge Pen
W.H. Smith, High Street stationers.

Lined Paper
Early Learning Centres.
Philip and Tacey Ltd., Northway, Andover, Hampshire SP10 5BA.
Taskmaster Ltd., Morris Road, Leicester LE2 6BR
Tel: 0116 270 4286
Email: taskmast@webleicester.co.uk
W.H. Smith, High Street stores.

Pencil Holders
LDA, Abbeygate House, East Road, Cambridge CB1 1DB
Tel: 01223 365445
Email: ldaorders@compuserve.com

Bibliography

Alston, J. and Taylor, J. (1987) *Handwriting: Theory, Research and Practice*. Routledge: London.

Alston, J. (1990) *Writing Left-handed*. Dextral Books: Manchester.

Alston, J. (2000) *Teaching Spelling: A Guide for Teachers and Parents*. QEd Publications: Lichfield.

Assessment of Performance Unit (1991) *Assessment Matters: No.4. Language for Learning*. School Examinations and Assessment Council: London.

Cato, V., Fernandes, C., Gorman, T., Kispal, A. and White, J. (1992) *The Teaching of Initial Literacy: How do teachers do it?* NFER: Slough.

Hamilton, M. (1987) *Literacy, Numeracy and Adults: Evidence from the National Child Development Study*. ALBSU: London.

Jarman, C. (1993) *The Development of Handwriting Skills*. Stanley Thornes: Cheltenham.

McNally, J. and Murray, W. (1962) *Key Words to literacy and the teaching of reading*. The Teacher Publishing Co: Kettering.

Rubin, N. and Henderson, S.E. (1982) 'Two Sides of the Same Coin: Variations in Teaching Methods and Failure to Learn to Write.' *Special Education: Forward Trends*. Vol 9, 4, pp.17-24.

Wallis Myers, P. (1994) *The Animal Alphabet Story Book and Large Moveable Letters*. Bowden.

Useful Addresses

Basic Skills Agency, Commonwealth House, 1-19 New Oxford Street, London WC1A 1NU.
Tel: 020 7405 4017
Email: enquiries@basic-skills.co.uk

British Dyslexia Association, 98 London Road, Reading RG1 5AU
Tel: 0118 966 2677
Web site: www.bda-dyslexia.org.uk

DfEE, Sanctuary Buildings, Great Smith Street, Westminster, London SW1P 3BT
Tel: 0870 000 2288
Web site: www.dfee.gov.uk
Email: info@dfee.gov.uk

Dyslexia Institute, 133 Gresham Road, Staines, Middlesex TW18 2AJ
Tel: 01784 463 851
Web site: www.dyslexia-inst.org.uk

Dyspraxia Foundation, 8 West Alley, Hitchin, Herts. SG15 1EG
Tel: 01462 454 986
Email: dyspraxiafoundation@hotmail.com
Web site: emmbrook.demon.co.uk/dysprax/homepage.htm

Handwriting Interest Group, Secretary: Felicitie Barnes, 6 Fyfield Road, Ongar, Essex CM5 OAH

The National Association for Special Educational Needs (NASEN), 4/5 Amber Business Village, Amber Close, Tamworth B77 4RP
Tel: 0800 018 2998
Email: welcome@nasen.org.uk
Web site: www.nasen.org.uk

National Children's Bureau, 8 Wakley Street, London EC1V 7QE
Tel: 020 7843 6000
Web site: www.ncb.org.uk

Qualifications and Curriculum Authority (QCA), 29 Bolton Street, London
W1Y 7PD
Tel: 020 7509 5555
Web site: www.qca.org.uk

Maths.